HABITAT DESTRUCTION

by

Harriet Brundle

CLIMATE CHANGE

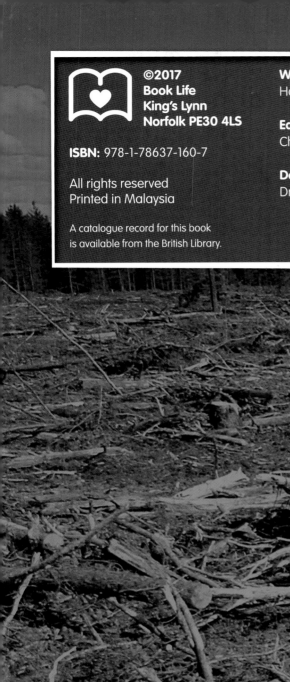

©2017
Book Life
King's Lynn
Norfolk PE30 4LS

Written by:
Harriet Brundle

ISBN: 978-1-78637-160-7

Edited by:
Charlie Ogden

All rights reserved
Printed in Malaysia

Designed by:
Drue Rintoul

A catalogue record for this book
is available from the British Library.

CONTENTS

Words in **bold** are explained in the glossary on page 31.

WHAT IS CLIMATE CHANGE?

KEY TERMS

- The <u>weather</u> is the day-to-day changes we see and feel outside. For example, the weather may be sunny in the morning and raining in the afternoon.

- The <u>climate</u> is the usual weather in a place over a longer period of time. For example, Antarctica has an extremely cold climate for most of the year.

- <u>Climate change</u> is the long-term change in the climate and usual weather patterns of an area. Climate change usually affects very large areas. It could be a change in the amount of rainfall or the average temperature of an area.

Tropical Climate

Arctic Climate

Earth's climate is always changing. Over the last 4.5 billion years, Earth has experienced both very hot and very cold climates. For the last 11,000 years, Earth's climate has stayed at a stable temperature of around 14 °C. However, in recent years this average temperature has been slowly increasing.

Why Might a Climate Change?

There are many different reasons for why a climate might change.

Some climate changes throughout history have had natural causes, for example **volcanic eruptions**. However, research has shown that changes to the climate in recent years have not been entirely down to natural causes. It is thought that a process called global warming is largely responsible.

1 Humans use energy for many different reasons, for example to power cars and light bulbs. This energy is largely produced by burning coal, oil and natural gas. Together, these things are known as **fossil fuels**. When these fossil fuels are burnt, they release lots of different gases, which are known as 'greenhouse gases'. Possibly the worst of these greenhouse gases is carbon dioxide.

2 The Earth's **atmosphere** is a collection of different gases that surround the planet. The atmosphere allows light and heat from the Sun to pass through to Earth. This makes the planet warm. After this, some of the light and heat from the Sun bounces off the Earth, travels back through Earth's atmosphere and goes into outer space.

3 Greenhouse gases mix with the gases in Earth's atmosphere and stop the heat from the Sun bouncing back into outer space. Because of this, the heat gets trapped inside the Earth's atmosphere. As a result, the temperature on Earth is rising. The more greenhouse gases that are released into Earth's tmosphere, the hotter the Earth will become.

WHAT IS A HABITAT?

A plant's or animal's habitat is their home; it's the place where they naturally live. An animal's habitat usually helps it to survive by providing it with food, water, shelter and a safe place to raise its young. There are many different types of habitat around the world, such as ponds, woodlands and jungles.

Each **species** of animal has **adapted** special traits over time that makes them better suited for their environment. An example of such an adaptation can be seen in the African elephant, which has huge ears that it uses to stay cool in the dry heat of the African savannah. The elephant's ears are covered in blood vessels that carry hot blood from inside the body. As the elephant flaps its ears, the breeze cools the blood, which then returns back into the body and cools the elephant down.

As animals are so well-suited to their habitats, it can be very difficult for them to survive in different places.

A habitat can be very large or very small.

Some of the largest habitats in the world are in the ocean. Find out more about life under the sea on page 18.

Ecosystems

In every habitat there are lots of different animals and plants that must all **interact** with each other and with non-living parts of the environment, such as the weather. This is an ecosystem. A healthy ecosystem relies upon energy being passed from plants to animals and between different species of animals. This is called a food chain.

| Daffodil | Caterpillar | Frog | Bird | Fox |

This is an example of a food chain. The arrows point to the animal that feeds on the plant or animal in the previous stage.

It is important that ecosystems remain stable. If one part of an ecosystem is changed or disrupted, it can have an impact upon every **organism** in that ecosystem. For example, if the zebra's habitat in the African savannah was destroyed, the number of zebras would fall. With less zebras around, the number of lions would fall as the big cats would have fewer animals to hunt. With less lions around, more animals might feel safe enough to live on the open savannah. This shows how changing one part an ecosystem can lead to the whole ecosystem changing.

Within a habitat there can also be several microhabitats. Microhabitats are very tiny habitats where small creatures and plants live. One habitat can be home to hundreds of microhabitats, each of which will have slightly different conditions to the larger habitat.

WHAT IS HABITAT DESTRUCTION?

Habitat destruction is when a habitat becomes unable to support the species living in it due to the habitat being changed or destroyed. As a result, the animals living in the habitat can find it very difficult to survive. Both human and natural activity can be responsible for habitat destruction. Natural causes of habitat destruction include fires, floods, diseases, earthquakes and volcanic activity; however, many areas can eventually recover from these natural events.

Changing a habitat does not always lead to the habitat being destroyed. Habitats are always changing and, most of the time, they are able to deal with these changes. It is only when habitats change very quickly, such as when huge areas of forest are cut down by humans, that they are unable to deal with the changes, leading to habitat destruction.

Some studies suggest that around one million different plant and animal species will become extinct in the next fifty years as a result of habitat destruction.

Habitat Fragmentation

A different type of habit destruction is called habitat fragmentation. Fragmentation happens when a habitat is altered but not completely destroyed. For example, if a road were built through the middle of a habitat, it could cut the habitat in half. The animals may choose to always stay on one side of the road, never crossing the road to look for food on the other side. This is habitat fragmentation.

The IUCN, an organisation that tries to protect and **conserve** nature, has a list of species that it calls the 'red list'. All of the animals on this list are **endangered** and habitat destruction is believed to be one of their biggest threats.

HOW DOES CLIMATE CHANGE AFFECT HABITATS?

Climate change has had a range of effects on animal habitats around the world.

Ice around the North and South Poles has been melting in recent years due to global warming. This has made it difficult for the animals that live in these habitats to survive.

The melting ice adds more water into the oceans. This increase of water raises the sea level and destroys beach habitats. This means that animals that nest on beaches will have nowhere to give birth to their young, meaning that they could quickly become endangered.

A sea turtle laying her eggs in a nest in the sand.

Climate change could also cause more extreme weather conditions. For some parts of the world, severe **droughts** are becoming increasingly common. Droughts can kill the plant life that animals rely on for their food and water. As a result, these areas can become **uninhabitable** and their ecosystems can be destroyed.

Animal Migration

Warmer temperatures on Earth have disrupted the **migration** patterns of thousands of animals. Birds are one of the most common types of animal to migrate and they often use the temperature to tell them when they should begin their migration. The changes in Earth's temperature have caused migrating birds to begin their journeys at the wrong times. If birds migrate at the wrong time, they could end up arriving in their new habitat too soon.

Although animals can adapt to new environments over time, the effects of climate change are happening too quickly for animals to keep up. If the temperature on Earth rose by just 2.5 °C, between 20% and 30% of all the animal and plant species on the planet would be at risk of extinction. Since 1880, the average temperature on Earth has risen by an estimated 0.85 °C.

Migrating Birds

POLLUTION

*Pollution is the introduction of a harmful **substance** into an environment.*

Pollution comes in many different forms and both human and natural causes can lead to pollution. Pollution is extremely damaging to life on Earth and it is a leading cause of habitat destruction.

Air pollution, caused mainly by the burning of fossil fuels, contributes to the rising temperature on Earth. One direct result of this is the melting ice in the areas around the North and South Poles. The animals that live in these areas, such as polar bears and penguins, are finding it harder to survive as the size of their habitat becomes smaller. Polar bears hunt for food on the surface of the ice but as the ice melts away, they have less places to hunt. This makes it more difficult for them to catch food.

A polar bear trying to hunt.

Smoke from chimneys is a type of pollution.

Acid Rain

Acid rain occurs as a result of pollution. Acid rain is a harmful type of rain that is made when gases from burning fossil fuels build up in Earth's atmosphere and combine with rain water. The result of this is rain that is extremely harmful to natural environments. When acid rain falls on forests, it can damage or kill much of the plant life. If the acid rain falls into lakes, it can be extremely damaging for the animals and plants that live in the lake. It could even kill them. This could result in the complete destruction of the ecosystem within the habitat and around the lake.

Water is essential for plants and animals to survive; however, the quality of the water on Earth is getting worse as a result of pollution. As well as acid rain, man-made chemicals, rubbish and waste are being released into water sources all over the world and, as a result, habitats are being damaged. When a habitat is damaged by water pollution, it makes it difficult for the animals that live there to find clean water to drink. This can lead to a lot of animals dying.

This forest has been damaged by acid rain.

Water Pollution

LAND DESTRUCTION

In the last 100 years, the population on Earth has risen by over four billion people. Each one of those people needs space to live and food to eat. As a result, large areas of land that were previously home to plant and animal life have been destroyed to make way for the building of new homes and **facilities**. More space is also needed for farmers to grow more food.

In order to make space for the growing population, large areas of forest and woodland have been cut down. Over the years, this has damaged or destroyed the habitats of hundreds of different animals and plants. This process is called deforestation. On top of this, many of the trees that are cut down are burnt as fuel, which adds to the planet's air pollution problem and global warming.

Nowadays, areas of woodland can quickly be torn down and replaced with houses and roads. Animals that previously lived in these areas, such as foxes, squirrels and rabbits, are often forced to find new places to live that have food and are safe.

LITTER

CITY OF LONDON

Deforestation in Canada

Wetlands

Marshes

Wetlands are areas that are covered by water for large parts of the year. Wetland areas include **marshes**, rivers, lakes and ponds. These areas of land are home to a wide range of animals such as frogs, ducks and insects. Wetlands are also used by migrating birds as a safe place to rest and feed before they continue their journey.

Many of the wetland areas around the world have been drained of their water and turned into spaces for farming or houses. Animals living in wetland areas need the water to survive and so, when the water is drained away, they are forced to move away from their habitat. If they are unable to find a new habitat quickly, they could die.

Plants need water to live. If the water is drained from wetland areas, the plant life that relied on this supply of water is also affected.

AROUND HALF OF THE WORLD'S WETLAND AREAS HAVE DISAPPEARED SINCE 1900.

FORESTS

Forests are home to millions of species of animal and plant life. Many endangered species live in forest habitats. As well as providing homes for a huge range of animals, forests also help to reverse the effects of climate change. Plants absorb carbon dioxide, which is one of the most damaging greenhouse gases. In return, the plants give off oxygen, which all animals need in order to survive.

Deforestation is happening all over the world and at an extremely fast pace. While many countries around the world are trying to plant more trees, which is called **reforestation**, large areas of forest are still being lost every year. Deforestation has a huge impact on the area and many animals cannot survive this immediate loss of habitat. Deforestation is nearly always caused by humans, although fires do occasionally destroy large areas of woodland. The reason humans cut down such huge areas of forest is usually to collect the wood from the trees, which can be burnt as a fuel or used as building material. As well as this, the cleared land is often used for farming.

Forests are home to lots of different animals and plants.

IT IS ESTIMATED THAT AN AREA OF FOREST THE SIZE OF 48 FOOTBALL FIELDS IS LOST EVERY MINUTE TO DEFORESTATION.

Deforestation

The Amazon Rainforest

The Amazon rainforest in South America is the world's largest tropical rainforest. The rainforest covers over 5 million square kilometres and is believed to be home to 10% of all the animal species in the world. The rainforest is also home to over 40,000 different species of plant that thrive in the wet and hot conditions.

The Amazon has been badly affected by deforestation. In the last 40 years, an area of the Amazon rainforest the size of France has been lost due to deforestation. The deforestation has had devastating effects upon the ecosystems within the rainforest.

The removal of trees has also destroyed the rainforest's **canopy**. The canopy is very important as it blocks strong rays of sunlight during the day and helps to keep the forest warm during the night, which helps to maintain a stable temperature for the animals that live there. As more trees are removed, it becomes harder for the rainforest to maintain a stable temperature. This could make it difficult for the animals that live in the Amazon to survive.

UNDER THE SEA

Human activity is impacting upon life under the sea in many different ways. The most damaging of these is probably overfishing. Overfishing occurs when more fish are caught and removed from the sea than can be replaced through natural **reproduction**. As the population on Earth increases, so does the number of fish being caught. As a result, some species of fish, such as bluefin tuna, are now endangered species.

Some of the carbon dioxide that is released when fossil fuels are burnt gets absorbed into the ocean. Although this process helps to reduce the impact of carbon dioxide on the atmosphere, it has a damaging impact upon the ocean. As the carbon dioxide is absorbed, the water becomes more **acidic**. This process is called ocean acidification. An ocean that is more acidic than it should be could end up killing much of the plant and animal life that lives there.

A fishing port in England.

Coral Bleaching

Millions of species, including lobsters, clams, seahorses and sponges, live near to or in coral reefs. Coral reefs are usually very colourful. However, the corals themselves are naturally white. The corals get their colour from the **algae** that lives on them. Algae is the coral's main food source and without it, the coral cannot survive. As the temperature on Earth increases, so too does the temperature of the ocean.

The increased temperature often makes the coral unwell and causes it to push away the algae. Without the algae to give it colour, the coral is left white. This is why it's called coral bleaching. This process does not kill the coral straight away, but if the warmer temperatures continue over a long period of time, the coral will eventually die. This would mean that the animals that live in the coral reef would have nowhere to live.

Coral Bleaching

The Great Barrier Reef off the coast of Australia is the largest coral reef in the world. It is so big that it can be seen from space! The Great Barrier Reef has experienced extreme coral bleaching events before. In 2002, 60% of the coral reef was bleached due to the warm weather. Although most of it did recover, about 5% never recovered.

Coral reefs are famous for their beautiful colours.

CASE STUDY
ASIAN ELEPHANTS

Asian elephants are found in many different countries in Asia, including India and Sri Lanka. Asian elephants often live together in herds, meaning that they need a lot of space in which to live. They prefer woodland areas with warm, dry weather. These elephants are **herbivores**, feeding mainly on the long grass that grows between trees, as well as bark, leaves, roots and stems. They require as much as 150 kilograms of food per day to survive and must also drink at least once a day, which means that fresh water sources within their habitat are extremely important.

Due to their size, elephants do not have any natural **predators**. Despite this, the number of Asian elephants left in the wild is rapidly decreasing. The Asian elephant is described on the IUCN red list as 'endangered', which is the second most severe status that can be given to a species and suggests that the animal is likely to become extinct. The fact that these elephants are endangered is largely the result of human activity.

ASIAN ELEPHANTS ARE VERY SIMILAR TO AFRICAN ELEPHANTS, EXCEPT THEY HAVE SMALLER EARS AND A SHORTER TRUNK.

India

Sri Lanka

An Asian elephant with its calf.

A large amount of the Asian elephant's habitat has been lost because humans have built settlements on the land. Areas of woodland have been torn down to make way for homes, roads and services for the people who live in Asia. Much of the wood is taken away and used for fuel, while the long grass is removed or left to die. Wetlands are often filled in, meaning that sources of clean water are harder to find. All of this has meant that the Asian elephant's habitat has got a lot smaller and has become a lot harder to live in.

As a result of habitat destruction, Asian elephants now only inhabit 15% of the land that they used to live on. Elephants are very sociable animals, but since their habitat has been made smaller and divided up by busy roads, herds of elephants have found it much more difficult to interact with each other.

THERE ARE ONLY BETWEEN 40,000 TO 50,000 ASIAN ELEPHANTS LEFT IN THE WILD. ALTHOUGH THIS NUMBER MAY SOUND LARGE, THERE WERE ROUGHLY TWICE THIS MANY ASIAN ELEPHANT'S ALIVE 100 YEARS AGO.

MOUNTAIN GORILLAS

Mountain gorillas were first discovered in 1902. These gorillas have shorter arms than most apes, as well as thicker fur, which keeps them warm in the cold mountain areas that they call home. Mountain gorillas live in dense forests that are very high in the mountains. Mountain gorillas are found in two main locations - the Virunga Mountains in the Democratic Republic of Congo, Rwanda and Uganda and the Bwindi National Park in Uganda.

Mountain gorillas are herbivores, mostly eating bamboo, thistles and fruit. The gorillas require a large amount of food due to their size. Mountain gorillas have an extremely slow rate of reproduction. Females can only give birth every three or four years and have just one young at a time. As a result of this, if the population of mountain gorillas falls, it could take a very long time to increase their numbers again.

Democratic Republic of Congo (green), Rwanda (blue) and Uganda (red).

Infant Mountain Gorilla

THE AVERAGE MALE MOUNTAIN GORILLA CAN WEIGH AS MUCH AS 160 KILOGRAMS!

Since their discovery, the number of mountain gorillas has continued to fall. The main reason for this is human activity, as more than 100,000 people now live on land that used to be part of the mountain gorillas' habitat. In 2004, over 1,500 **hectares** of the gorillas' woodland habitat was cleared by people who wanted to build houses there. As more and more of the gorillas' habitat has been destroyed through deforestation, the gorillas have been forced to move further up the cold mountains.

A settlement on the Virunga Mountains in Uganda

The soil found in the Virunga Mountains is ideal for growing crops and, because of this, much of this land has been claimed for farming and producing food. As well as this, power companies are exploring the area hoping to find supplies of fossil fuels underground. Any discoveries could result in even more habitat loss for the gorillas.

AS A RESULT OF CONSERVATION WORK TO PROTECT WHAT IS LEFT OF THEIR NATURAL HABITAT, THE NUMBER OF WILD MOUNTAIN GORILLAS IS NOW BEGINNING TO INCREASE. FIND OUT MORE ABOUT CONSERVATION WORK ON PAGE 26.

Large areas of the Virunga Mountains are now used for farming.

WHAT HAPPENS WHEN A HABITAT IS GONE?

It is very important that animal habitats are looked after so that no species is forced into extinction. Over time, natural events can cause lots of animals to go extinct. Forest fires can burn away huge areas of woodland, volcanic eruptions can destroy whole islands and heat waves and ice ages can leave animals without enough food and water to survive. There will always be species that are about to go extinct, but we should do our best to protect them for as long as we can.

When an entire habitat is destroyed, the plants and animals that lived in that habitat are destroyed too. The most common reasons for this happening include climate change, pollution, land destruction, **poaching** and over-hunting. Together these things are putting a huge strain on life all over the planet. From polar bears in the Arctic to gorillas in Africa, all life on Earth is suffering because of the damage that humans have done, and are continuing to do, to the environment.

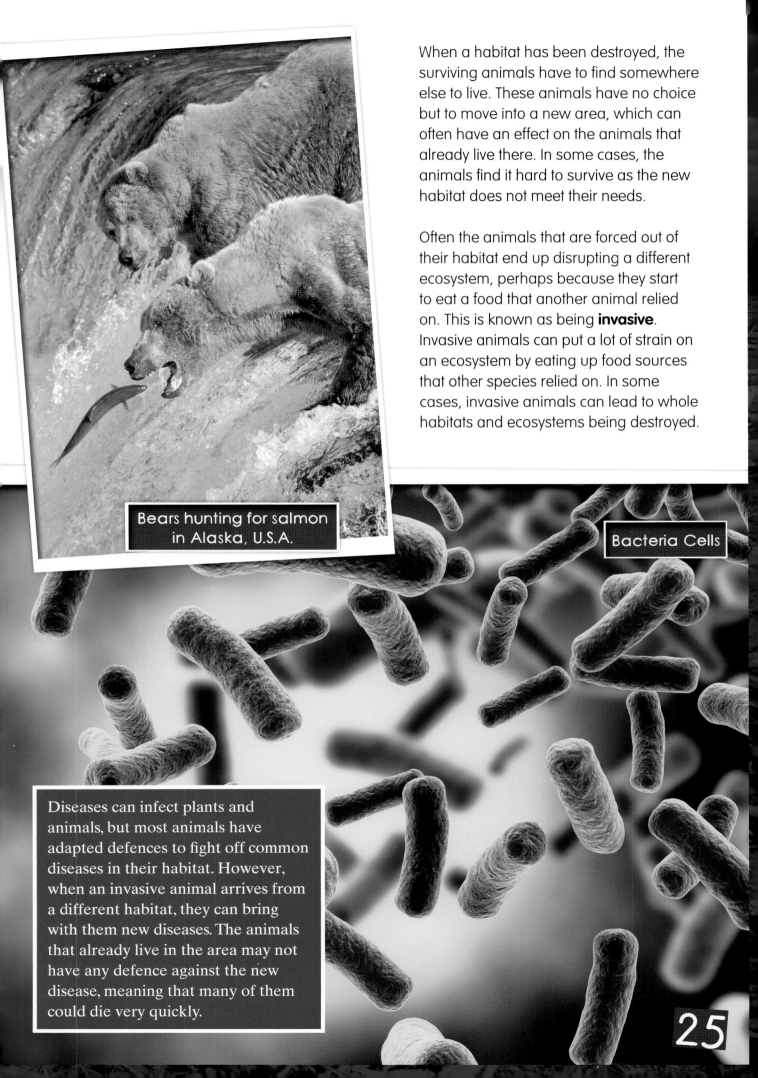

When a habitat has been destroyed, the surviving animals have to find somewhere else to live. These animals have no choice but to move into a new area, which can often have an effect on the animals that already live there. In some cases, the animals find it hard to survive as the new habitat does not meet their needs.

Often the animals that are forced out of their habitat end up disrupting a different ecosystem, perhaps because they start to eat a food that another animal relied on. This is known as being **invasive**. Invasive animals can put a lot of strain on an ecosystem by eating up food sources that other species relied on. In some cases, invasive animals can lead to whole habitats and ecosystems being destroyed.

Bears hunting for salmon in Alaska, U.S.A.

Bacteria Cells

Diseases can infect plants and animals, but most animals have adapted defences to fight off common diseases in their habitat. However, when an invasive animal arrives from a different habitat, they can bring with them new diseases. The animals that already live in the area may not have any defence against the new disease, meaning that many of them could die very quickly.

25

HABITAT PROTECTION

The protection of animal habitats from any further destruction is very important and many groups around the world are working to achieve this. They work to protect areas of land from being destroyed and the endangered species living there.

National parks and reserves have been established worldwide to offer a safe place for animals to live. These areas of land are protected by law, meaning that deforestation, poaching and building work are not allowed. Other areas, such as The Great Barrier Reef in Australia, have been protected by the same laws so that humans cannot fish or take naturally growing plant life from that area of the ocean. Some parks and reserves offer the opportunity for visitors to pay money to see the animals living there. This money goes towards maintaining the habitat.

Zion National Park, Utah, USA

People rafting on the Tara River in Durmitor National Park, Montenegro.

The World Wide Fund for Nature, often just called WWF, was established in 1961. It is a conservation group, meaning they work to protect animal species and their habitats by trying to reduce the harm of human activities on the environment. The group works in over 100 countries, making it the biggest conservation group in the world.

The WWF does lots of different things in order to protect wildlife and habitats around the world. They support **sustainable** methods of collecting wood, they help to stop illegal or dangerous fishing, they promote awareness of climate change and pollution and they help to fund conservation work around the world.

So far the WWF have run many successful campaigns to achieve these goals, such as reducing the amount of fishing in certain habitats, bringing a stop to companies looking for oil in the habitats of endangered species and stopping lots of large-scale deforestation.

There are many other groups, such as Greenpeace, The Nature Conservancy and Natural Resources Defence Council, who all work to protect wildlife and habitats from damage and destruction.

HOW CAN WE HELP?

There are lots of different ways that we can all help to stop habitat destruction.

1 Try to find out about the wildlife and habitats in your local area and consider getting involved with local conservation groups.

2 Tell your family and friends about climate change and how important it is to look after our planet. Also, try to get as many people as you can interested in helping to save the environment.

3 Recycle! It is important that we recycle as much as possible in order to reduce the amount of waste being put into landfill sites. Recycling can be done at home, at school and in the wider community, so try to make sure that anything you can recycle is taken to special recycling banks or is put in recycling bins.

4 Try not to be wasteful. Food waste also contributes to the waste being dumped in landfill sites, so try to reuse anything that doesn't need to be thrown away and make sure that food is eaten before it goes out of date.

5 Try to reduce the amount of fossil fuels that you use. Rather than using the car, try to walk or cycle to where you need to go. If you have to use a car, try sharing with others who are also going to the same place. You could also turn down the heating at home and wear more layers of clothing to stay warm instead.

6 Plant a tree! Trees absorb some of the greenhouse gases that cause climate change and give off oxygen. The more trees that are planted, the better!

The WWF hold 'Earth Hour' every year. On the last Saturday in March, everyone who is taking part turns off the lights in their house for one hour between 8.30pm and 9.30pm. The WWF hope that this act will show how much people care about the planet. Why not join in and turn off your lights for an hour?

USEFUL WEBSITES

To find out more about the work of the WWF, go to: www.wwf.org.uk. Click on the tab that says "get involved" to find out what you could do to help!

Visit www.icun.org to discover how the IUCN help to protect animal homes.

Learn how to better reduce, reuse and recycle your rubbish with this site: www.recycling-guide.org.uk

Use this informative website climatekids.nasa.gov to learn all about climate change. Click on the "play" tab to play games as you learn.

Go to www.earthtimes.org for interesting blogs and pages that are filled with environmentally-friendly ideas and tips.

To discover more about Greenpeace, visit www.greenpeace.org/international

Visit www.nature.org to find out about The Nature Conservancy. Go to the "where we work" section to find out about conservation work that's happening near to you.

GLOSSARY

acidic	containing a lot of acid
adapted	changed over time to suit different conditions
algae	living things that are like plants, but have no roots, stems, leaves or flowers
atmosphere	the mixture of gases that make up the air and surround the Earth
canopy	the top layer of branches in a forest
conserve	protect from damage or harm
droughts	long periods of very little rainfall, which lead to a lack of water
endangered	when a species of animal is in danger of becoming extinct
extinct	a species of animal that is no longer alive
facilities	buildings or pieces of equipment provided for a specific purpose
fossil fuels	fuels, such as coal, oil and gas, that formed millions of years ago from the remains of animals and plants
hectares	a unit of measurement equal to 10,000 square metres
herbivores	animals that only eat plants
interact	be involved or communicate with another creature
invasive	spreading quickly and causing harm
marshes	ground near a river, lake or the sea that is always wet and often floods
migration	the seasonal movement of animals from one area to another
organism	a living thing
poaching	catching and killing animals without permission
predators	animals that hunt other animals for food
reforestation	planting trees
reproduction	the process of having young
species	a group of very similar animals or plants that are capable of producing young together
substance	something with physical properties
sustainable	able to continue over a period of time
uninhabitable	not suitable to live in

INDEX